CONDITIONAL

FUTURE

PERFECT

CONDITIONAL

FUTURE

PERFECT

dan curley

Volume editor, John Cassels
Cover illustration by S.L. Johnson
SLJohnsonImages.com
Interior design by Sky Santiago

ISBN: 9781950066001

Wolfson Press
Master of Liberal Studies Program
Indiana University South Bend
1700 Mishawaka Avenue
South Bend, Indiana 46634-7111
WolfsonPress.com

TO THE MEMORY OF MY PARENTS
I begin to understand you, now.

CONTENTS

III

FOREWORD
No Things But in Tangents

I have known Dan Curley since we were both undergraduates. In those days—
fully three decades ago—I knew him as an antically poetic soul but not as a
poet per se. He *did* compose lyrics for rock songs, but my extravagantly blunt
assessment of one of these efforts placed me in the critical company of the
speaker of his poem "I Wish": "I wish I hadn't said / What I said—take your
pick— / But I wouldn't wish to unsay it / Except for when I critiqued my
daughter / And she vowed never to sing to me again." A little later, we worked
together on some translations of Catullus, an enthusiasm I had gotten by way
of Frank O'Hara and Dan had come by more honestly as a classics student.
Still, when the poems from which this volume is drawn began popping into
the world via social media a few years ago, it was a bracing surprise—not so
much *that* Dan was writing poems (for all I knew, he had been all along) but
that the poems he was now sharing were so distinctive and accomplished, that
he seemed to be emerging so close to fully formed.

Much toil underlies such an illusion, of course—among it, in Dan's
case, many years as a teacher and scholar of Latin language and literature—
but the story of Dan's "birth" as poet, as he eventually relayed it to me, is
appealingly straightforward and unpretentious: Having spent much of his
professional life studying and teaching poetry, he thought he ought to give
the writing of it a try. The opening poem of Conditional Future Perfect
discloses, in deceptive miniature, a great deal of what made that attempt
such a good idea. "Tangential" is both an introduction (to the book, to the
poet and some of his typical concerns) and a statement of purpose. The
speaker's wife says that he goes "off on tangents"; he prefers the term "lateral
thinking in action" and volunteers a practical, problem-solving example:

How else would

I have remembered the pork chops
Were left in the car if not for our
Starveling child making BLTs

For lunch?

The solution to the problem may just reveal another problem (spoiled chops),
but the speaker is already off onto a slice of hackneyed poesy that somehow
counts as "the family motto"—"When a task / Is once begun / Never leave it 'til /
It's done"—and then another tangent:

<blockquote>

                  but now here's the cat
     Tossing me come-hither looks,
     Rubbing her cheek and ear against

     The door frame. How essential
     To run fingers through the fur, over
     The arching back and up the victory

     Column of the tail!

</blockquote>

This task is, of course, nothing like "essential"; it seems so only in the exuberant, slightly overheated rendering of the scene (of which the word "essential" is itself an essential—emblematic—component, one that both takes out and reinstates itself).

To pause here, one of the crucial things to be said about *Conditional Future Perfect* is that it is consistently, delightfully amusing. Its humor inheres, in places, in deadpan reactions (of, e.g., the errant, checkpoint-avoiding speaker of "The Night We Ran the Blockade")—

<blockquote>

              Plan was,
     Go the long way around, but
     The backass country roads
     Led us astray,

             which we grasped
     When we saw the lake
     Roiling under the waxing moon. Shit,
     It's the lake! I said.

</blockquote>

—and in others in nutty conceits (e.g., "Uncovering Howard," a masterful, irreverent elegy for Howard Nemerov) but *everywhere* in the poet's lambent, just-hyperbolic-enough voice—a sweet spot to which Curley has preternatural access. The speaker of these poems is an educated, garrulous everyman who wears his learning lightly while sparing the world he confronts—be it social (wife, child, students, colleagues) or physical (broken chairs, old barns, airport interiors)—none of it. Least spared is his own person(a), his attempts at understanding experience mixing up joy, anxiety, and (always) rueful self-awareness. Sustaining such a tone may seem an easy thing to do in the confines of a brief lyric; it isn't, but it is *vexingly* more difficult in a capacious context like that of this volume's bravura title poem, one of several elaborative set pieces (Curley's way with the long list calls to mind the work of, among others, Kenneth Koch). "Tangential" ends:

My wife says
I've been on tangents ever since
I came out of the womb. I say
Being born was the tangent. I've
Made a life trying to get back
To what I was doing before that.

So deftly is the reversal deployed that it is tempting to regard it as merely clever and not take the claim seriously. Knowing the speaker to be a Latin scholar, one might see Lucretius here, pulling back the curtain and waving. But this is more than just to say, "Well, I didn't mind not existing for an eternity before I was born, so I don't mind the idea of not existing again." *Fear* of death isn't the issue; indeed, for a funny book, *Conditional Future Perfect* is notably preoccupied with death and/or disaster, but not in a haunted or shrinking way. The deepening shadow that mortality casts over the book's third section, in particular the extraordinary elegies toward its end, is lightened—made bearable—by how *tough* these poems are. The poet never mistakes his grief for the grief of his subjects, loving them enough (to paraphrase "David,") to let them pass.

Nonexistence ("what I was doing before"), far from constituting a harm, is an inevitable *goal*. One makes one's life "trying to get back" to it. No things but in tangents, so tangents are essential. And this valuation implies no death wish—it merely sets a boundary and says, "This mess *here* constitutes the way back. Try to make something of it. At least pay attention." Or you may find yourself, at the end of the world, as the speaker of "My Brave Last Days" imagines, "stupidly" attempting a repair that should have been made long ago ("There're some loose shingles . . . / I've been meaning to replace").

If something besides death haunts *Conditional Future Perfect*, it is the proverbial unfinished task of the Curley family motto. Not even a seventh-grader who once bluffed her way through a book report can escape. In "The Chronicles of Yolanda," the title figure makes a bullshit presentation on C. S. Lewis's *The Magician's Nephew*, unaware that most of the class, which she joined just the year before, had been primed by an earlier teacher to see through this effort:

I told Yolanda I thought she was
A beautiful faker, but Bridget was having
None of it: This was Robert Lewis, the son,
And a totally different book,
So I should shut my stupid face.

If you see Yolanda, please tell her
She owes a book report. Mention how
The way of academia is to purchase redemption,
At cost. Tell her I ought to know.

There is perhaps a faint Catullan echo in "If you see Yolanda, please tell her," but more importantly, so much of adult life—academic conflict, erotic conflict, deception, complicity—is here, itching to strut its stuff on the adult stage, and the speaker, to whom it *has* now happened, characteristically just wants to share his knowledge. Not that it will save anybody, but knowing you are not saved counts for something too, is a kind of release.

When Dan turned in the manuscript of this book, it was 173 pages long—approximately 150 poems. Helping to hone that bulk to its present form has been one of the pleasures of my life. It has taken too long, but now the task is accomplished. Dan shares with Frank O'Hara a prolific bent and, to a certain extent, a focus on the individual poem—the phenomenology of its creation—that crowds out subsequent, curatorial concerns; as the speaker of "My Brave Last Days" confesses, "I've never been / A big-picture kind of guy." He's already written at least another book. And I realize that I haven't said *anything* about the lovely second section of this book, a travelogue of sorts, nearly all of the poems taking place in Italy, which Dan visits often (Rome in particular, frequently in the company of students). Nor have I mentioned the alarming schematic breakdown of the final poem, "Toward a Grammar of Death," or a hundred other things. That's okay, though—you will find them (and they you). I'm not off the hook by any means, but it's not the end of the world.

John Cassels
Silver Spring, Maryland

I

TANGENTIAL

I go off on tangents, my wife says,
But I prefer to call them lateral
Thinking in action. How else would

I have remembered the pork chops
Were left in the car if not for our
Starveling child making BLTs

For lunch? Sure, there's something
To the family motto—When a task
Is once begun / Never leave it 'til

It's done—but now here's the cat
Tossing me come-hither looks,
Rubbing her cheek and ear against

The door frame. How essential
To run fingers through the fur, over
The arching back and up the victory

Column of the tail! My wife says
I've been on tangents ever since
I came out of the womb. I say

Being born was the tangent. I've
Made a life trying to get back
To what I was doing before that.

AUTONYMY

If I should be an autobiographer,
I would work in the third person
And write, He was kind to animals,
The implication being that he, a

Charmer of malcontent felines and
Friend to the neighbor's rooster,
Was good. But it cuts both ways:
If there're more receipts for the

Veterinarian than for charities,
The biographer must ask how his
Subject could call himself a humanist.
I had a friend (still do) who claimed

Autonomy was the capacity to name
The self—that would be autonymy,
But it seemed right to us, being tall
Drinks of water in our time though

Far from masters of ourselves. It's
The fine line between becoming
And having become, between being
Vincent and bragging, or at least

Believing, to have been Victor.

THE NIGHT WE RAN THE BLOCKADE

They put up a checkpoint.
We saw it at a distance driving home,

Red and blue scars on the horizon.
The closer we crept,

    the weirder I got:
What if I refused to answer or,
Screwing up dumb nerve, blurted,
What's it to ya?

    The whole thing stank,
So we pulled a U-turn out of the line
And doubled back. Plan was,
Go the long way around, but
The backass country roads
Led us astray,

   which we grasped
When we saw the lake
Roiling under the waxing moon. Shit,
It's the lake! I said.

   Truth to tell,
It was beautiful to cross the bridge in silence,
Over houses sunk in the last century's floods,
Tires groaning the requiem of homeowners

Drowned in the making of the lake,
Progress yielding to progress:

Pass over, moonlit scofflaws!
Pass over or tender yourselves to us,
Lost and under water.

THE CHRONICLES OF YOLANDA

In the seventh grade Yolanda reported on
The Magician's Nephew. She brought
The children to the pool's edge,

The brink of ruddy Charn and the cruel queen's
Palace. They were about to jump into the pool
(She said) when they heard a lion's
Roar. It frightened them, but with help from
A talking owl they escaped from Narnia
And made it back safe to London.
She really enjoyed this book.

O Yolanda! you came to our school
In the sixth grade—and you weren't there
In the fifth when Miss Cooper read to us,
Planted Narnia in our imaginations.
She tabulated Aslan and raised him up.
She made all the horses take wing.

I told Yolanda I thought she was
A beautiful faker, but Bridget was having
None of it: This was Robert Lewis, the son,
And a totally different book,
So I should shut my stupid face.

If you see Yolanda, please tell her
She owes a book report. Mention how
The way of academia is to purchase redemption,
At cost. Tell her I ought to know.

THE FREE SALE

Walking our five-mile loop, about twenty
Minutes out, we saw a rocking chair,
A pair of rakes, and a sign saying:
FREE. They are my people, the free-
Sellers of the world, and, having learned
Something from twelve years
Of home ownership, I went over
For a better look at the chair.
(Not the rakes—we're flush with rakes.)
It seemed sturdy, but it was encrusted

With brown paint, flaking and squalid.
It could be restored, I said, taking a
Neutral tone, but you were intrigued,
As I knew you'd be, because a wrap-around
Porch, abundant with rocking chairs, is first
On your list of home-reno dreams. . . .
The miles crept by. I began to get
Tired—pounding pavement is hard on my
Knees, and, though I generally prefer biking,

I'd rather spend the time with you,
Who prefer hiking—as we contemplated dinner.
An idyllic discourse on tuna melts turned,
In the fragrant afternoon, to the
Possibility of grilled chicken with zucchini and
The question of whether any potatoes were
Left over. Then, after I'd consented to
Drive to town and see what the

Grocery store had, you gave me a
Choice: Drive back and get the chair or—
God, no more chairs! I blurted.
I pleaded my case in the fumbling
Way I do when we disagree, and
I made you angry. You couldn't feel
The aching in my knees or know

The aching in my chest from the
Failed projects of the prior decade,
Not least being the long-
Neglected armchair I bargained hard for
At the old flea market with an eye toward
Refinishing it and, after commissioning new

Cushions from your mother, retiring to indolence
Of the highest order. Another chair
To restore—impossible! And if they matter
So much, why did we get rid of
The rocking chair that calmed our colicky

Baby in the free sale we had
Before moving cross-country? I didn't ask,
Because I am not a maniac.
I phoned our baby, now a driver,

To pick me up. You kept walking, and we passed
You marching down the hill. Well,
She said, let's look (the sweet, solicitous child),

And drove to the place this comedy
Began. Of course, we found nothing there—

Neither sign nor rakes nor rocking chair.

IN THE CASCADES

In the Cascades there are no waterfalls
To compare with your tears. Wait—
Don't shroud your hand in your sleeve.
Let them pour down until I promise

We'll go back, braving the treacherous
Pass, and find your mother's pen,
Which fell between the nightstand
And the bed when I distracted you

From your notes. Maybe housekeeping
Found it and took it to the front desk.
Maybe it's the offering due for a night
Alone, a sacrifice to the desolate ghost

Of our working lives.

CURLEY'S THEME

May a horn play an unassuming C
Before rising to F on gossamer strings
And unfolding its charms from there.
Should my wife take a lover while I'm
Away, may the theme broadcast my
Return, all shrieks and timpani. May
She whisper, Curley, and may
Her lover clamber out the window
Onto the roof and break a lecherous leg.
May it be a fanfare of brass when I
Enter the classroom, the students
Finishing texts with a hasty
DCURLZ and standing at attention.
As I deliver the oration of my career
On the faculty floor, may it kick in
Midway through, crescendoing into
A soaring refrain. May it guide me
Exhausted to my seat as colleagues
Start to applaud, roars of Curley! Curley!
Almost drowning out my leitmotif.
May variations on my theme cue
Every crucial moment of my life.
On my deathbed may it take a minor
Key, slow, stately, enough to dampen
The clicks and beeps of the monitors,
While I clasp hands with nearest and
Dearest. May it conclude on a single,
Keening note, a violin sustaining the
Harp's arpeggio, as everything fades
To black and the credits roll. Later
Download it onto your heart, play it
When you have a bottle between you
And someone you love. Drink up,
O my auditors.

MAKE A CULTURE OF LAUGHING

Make a culture of laughing. I'll make one of
Listening, learning your cadence and timbre
By heart.

       Let's make a culture of hiding,
Being missed after getting long gone.

                   I'll make a
Culture of roving but returning. You make one of
Receiving me not because you must but
If you will.

       Let's make a culture of culture and become
Theorists of our age: I'll take Cryptolocality and
Ecomodernity, because you despise them.

Make a culture of kissing. I'll make one of
Kissing back. Let's reject the culture of shame and
Embrace the culture of sex in the shower.

We'll make a culture of culturing milk and
Donate all proceeds to other cultures.

I'll make a culture of praise, if you make one of
Blame. We'll eschew the culture of cults
But not kilts.

       When you make a culture of crying,
I'll make one of drying your tears: See
How I hold my kerchief by the corner and
Dab just so?

       We'll make a culture of
Gardening, our hands planted in earth,
So long as we make a concurrent culture of
Weekends sleeping in.

       Let's make a culture of
You and then of me, and make of us
One true culture

    and throw it open to culturists
Everywhere. You make a culture of handing out
Grants to study our culture. I'll make a culture of
Preserving the research.

      And after our
Culture's vetted and secure, let's unmake
The very culture of culture-making

With a culture of revolution.

E.G.

I'm less wasteful of late, reusing minor items of
Plastic, such as forks, realigning entire categories,
Such as those whose rubric is Waste, under which
Rubric used to reside the dirt on my hands,
Henceforth to be called soil in recognition of its
Vitality, its necessity. The foothill soil is fine and
Ferrous, imparting mineral essence to my food,
Such as a sandwich, when I neglect to wash
My hands after working the soil, the water
Conserved for something more useful, such as
Soaking the garden beds, whose soils produce
Both food and flowers, which are under the rubric
Nourishment. The former nourish my body,
The latter my eyes, which are not under the rubric
Body but belong to a category to be determined,
One including all the things that drive my woman
Wild, such as a proper pasta Bolognese, teeth
Grazing the ridge of an ear, soil on my hands.

THE STAR WARS

I used to holler, What's new,
Magoo? and give some part of
Your person a tweak.
It was charming until it wasn't,

Until it was again, *ad nauseam*,
Like some Finns we used to know
Who couldn't get a handle on
The definite article, ever asking

Were we going to *The Star Wars*?
Or phoning hours late to say
They were stuck on The Aurora,
Which avenue was (fair enough)

In those days nowhere nobody
Wanted to be, not even seasoned
Scandinavians grown up among
Hash bars and needle parks.

Their strangeness was a nudity
They covered with extraneous
Syllables, each The the skimpy
Preserver of modesty, a thong

Hiding pudenda or tendering
Straps from low-rise jeans
To assure all of The America
We are here, we come in peace.

SHOVELING THE DRIVEWAY WITH YOU

The night before the snowstorm, daughter,
We spoke of your poetry class and the tropes
Of reading aloud, such as the art of the intro:
And this is a poem about grief (you croaked

Into your fist) called "Dead Dog Tornado,"
While I marveled at the voice within you
That conjured so fine a collocation so
Naturally. The night of the snowstorm

You phoned me from the street, the plow
Having sealed off the driveway. Meeting on the
Porch where the shovels are, we made short
Work of it: you, the perimeter; I, the side-

To-side. I was not quite young, but far less
Old than I had been, taking my pills before
Bedtime. I feel a poem coming on, I said.
I'll call it "Shoveling the Driveway with You."

"Dead Dog Tornado," you said, brushing
Your sleeves clean of snow.

NOTHING NEW UNDER THE SUN

Which Renaissance lunatic sent you to me?
Because you clearly don't belong here.

It's your faith in humanity betrays you
And the fact that you can't use the internet

Worth a damn. Say *piacere* to Leonardo,
When next you see him, and let go the mouse,

Which is neither a weapon nor a transmitter
To the old masters. No, I don't know why

They did what they did, your colleagues
At the Health Department, as your *colleghi*

At the Fullers' Guild must have done, too,
But for being cowed by a woman of sense

And scruples: *sub sole nihil novum.* No,
I don't know why that page timed out

Again. Yes, I will love you until I die.

I WISH

This fly would cease its frenzied
Buzzing against the cellophane. And I wish
The cat would realize my anguish
And dispatch the crazy son of a bitch—
A leap, a snap of jaws,
A loyal show of atrocity and grace.

I wish I had an elite corps of kitties
In smart little vests: the Feline Force,
Scourge of the mouse-infested office,
Saviors of lost children!

       I wish corporations
Were corporeal so as to be invited
For drinks, made to admit that no one
Needs that much money, and be stuck
With the tab.

     I wish I hadn't said
What I said—take your pick—
But I wouldn't wish to unsay it
Except for when I critiqued my daughter
And she vowed never to sing to me again—
A pity, because her tones are pure
As my wishes are sincere, and I wish
She'd entrust her voice to my hearing
Just once.

    I wish the error precipitating Ovid's
Exile were as senseless and stark as being
Struck by a dune buggy on a dusky beach.

I wish a librarian had cherished Sophocles
As much as Euripides—enough to have
Smuggled the tau-volume home in his cloak
The night before the library burned
And the city tore itself to pieces;
To have tucked, during the devastation,
The poet into a party wall crevice
With a prayer for his recovery—
So that I might be certain of what
Tereus did to poor Philomela and how she

And her sister exacted their revenge
(Revenge), however much one, after learning,
Might wish to unlearn it.

                    I wish I'd been a better
Student of Greek, but I took it up at a time
When my heart was bursting with wishes,
Mastering the Attic dialect not among
Their number.

           The girl who rescued me
In those torpid moments after my ex
Became my ex and put me on the first bus
Leaving town, who talked to me despite my
Union Jack shirt and stupid, torn-up jeans
And lunatic tears (or because of the tears),
Who called me Boy and schooled me in jazz
And made me wish Milwaukee would never arrive—
I wish I could remember her name.

I wish this poem had less substance,
More bite. I wish it were sharper than it is.
Its readers might wish the same, and

                         my last wish
Is for you, that you achieve your dearest wish.
Don't say what it is, only promise it's ethical.
Matter of fact, by reading thus far you've
Already promised, and you further agree
To hold me harmless for wishing you well,
Which might go against your wishes,
But tough titty (said the kitty).

THE ROAD TRIP

Began when I smashed a carton of eggs
During brunch, an hour before we were
To meet downstairs, pile into the car,
And drive four-plus hours to investigate
Another car. Next, I gashed my lip shaving.
The clotting cost almost twenty minutes,
Tissue dangling from my chin—and this
An echo of the tissue stuck to my wrist
After the cat scratched me in the night.
Ten miles out we bore down on a bird,
A sparrow, though in hindsight its dappled
Coat bespoke another species. Bird!
My daughter cried (an apt summation)
But there was no room to maneuver, no
Chance of slowing. We had every hope
The thing would take (A) notice and
(B) wing, like crows pecking at roadkill
Launching themselves as traffic approaches
Then landing in the wake and resuming
The feast, but the poor bastard stayed put,
Turning its head to meet us at the last.
My wife tried to align car with *corpus*
And keep the bird between the wheels,
But the updraft was strong. All parties
Agreed a feathery something was left,
Mother vowing, as only a kid raised on
Jonathan Livingston Seagull would, it was
Stunned (He was moving. Gliding.),
Daughter shaking her head and conjuring
Crows devouring fresh kill. We recalled
Our previous victims: squirrels, mainly,
The occasional rabbit; something dark
In my memory insisted I once hit a stray
Cat, but I shrugged it off. The very worst,
We concurred, are deer. At some point
Carcolepsy overtook the child, leaving
Her parents to carry on as suited each's
Nature—hers quiet, contemplative steering,
His raucous parades of road signs read
In tongues and rounds of corrupted
Pop songs (Motownkaitlin's back again!).
You're so damn noisy, my wife shouted,

You silence-murderer! I wrote that down,
Adding: Guilty as charged, blood on hands.

MY BRAVE LAST DAYS

When the world is ending
We won't know it. By the time they get around
To drawing a red line under the date,
It'll be too late,
Assuming anyone's left to work a pen.

Some say dangling modifiers
Are the end of the world. I say
It's the split
Infinitive, which is every bit as dangerous
As splitting an atom and far easier
To actually do.

The fission of grammar
Requires a zealous conviction. One has to go for it
Wholeheartedly, just as Bono knows
No problem worth solving
Should be solved without the falsetto.

How to lean into my brave last days?
There're some loose shingles on the barn
I've been meaning to replace.
Were the doors not frozen shut,
Were I able to reach my ladder,

I think I'd tackle that project.
It sounds pointless in the face of Armageddon,
But I've never been
A big-picture kind of guy,
And they bother me every time
I drive past,

Those tattered,
Ectopic strips of asphalt,

Ascending to which is courage enough.
Heights were my forte, once,
But lately the *ahem*
Of gravity gives me a tingle

Behind the knees. It's not fright
So much as realizing I

Have more to lose than I used to.
When you're ten years old,
Straddling the chimney of your house

With a pair of binoculars, and you die,
It's hard on your parents
But glorious for you.
When your life flashes before your eyes,

It's brief
(Unless your life had Sawyeresque proportions),

And you can get back to cherishing
The business of falling: the speed of it
And all that excellent air.
There's no time
To regret everything you'll miss out on,
Like losing your virginity
Or getting your license (the same day,
Had you played your cards right),
And quite possibly your falling

Is an escape from being poor
Or being bullied
Or abused,
In which cases the approaching ground
Ought to be a comfort.

You die a hero's death.
But at my age you're a fool
Who should've known better
Than to stupidly fix up his barn
At the end of the world.

CONDITIONAL FUTURE PERFECT

Should you, darling, predecease me, and should anyone at the funeral
Ask what you were like (better to write, What you

Are like, because you are, in fact, with me still, and
To think of you, as sometimes I do, in the conditional

Future perfect is less depressing than confusing. Note:
Do I describe her as she was hours ago—sleeping, now, while

I churn this out—or do I transfer her current character
To a postmortem imaginary in the hope that it will possess

Not truth, which is elusive, but at least veracity, a semblance
Of the self in the, hopefully far-off, future?), I'd say

(Taking the latter route and answering the question of what you were like),
She was a slow eater. Which means exactly what it is

And no double entendre. Whether dining out or dining in,
You eat with meticulous precision, bringing the protein

Into line with the starch and alternating from bites of these
To bites of the vegetable in a ratio whose calculus has long

Frustrated me, and always (always) working from worst
To best, either in flavor or consistency or whatever criteria make

Sense on the plate. Which is all very efficient (not for
Nothing are you an engineer from a family of engineers),

And one might think such efficiency would yield faster, not slower,
Eating, but one would be mistaken, since your system maximizes not only

Efficiency but also enjoyment of the food at hand, which yields
Slower, not faster, eating. Ah! I seem an ungrateful, unworthy

Churl, as if I took no pleasure in breaking bread with
My woman, when the opposite is the case. There are

Few things I cherish more than sitting down with you to
Eat; even a bowl of cereal becomes a sumptuous banquet. What

Is more, I've gone and gotten myself caught in the bear
Trap of sentiment, imagining I'm bereft of my beloved, pretending she's

Transmigrated to planes too remote for mundane tributes to
Slow eating and whatnot to reach, when she is alive and

Warm and asleep in the room next door—Oh, I hear
You stirring now, soon to have thrown off the covers and

Sat up and swung your legs over the side of the
Bed and stretched and dressed and found your way downstairs

And poured yourself a glass of ice with juice in it,
Which will have staved off your hunger an hour

Or two, enough to get a little work done in your
Study (which will have become cozy, because I turned on the

Heat for you), until it's time for breakfast or, probably,
Brunch, which we will have eaten *entre nous*. The trap is

Not that you'll read what's written here (but it might come
To that—see below), since as a rule I don't share

Poems with you, not even when you're in them. Rather, that
Someone else will have read it and remembered it, and,

Next time we're out to dinner with them, they'll weigh its
Veracity by watching you eat. And if you will have eaten

Perceptibly slowly, they'll look at me and smile, and I'll have
To smile back, because any other gesture (like shaking my head

Or drawing a finger across my throat with a *Hhhkk!*) will have
Caught your eye, despite your being engrossed in eating,

As you likely would be. Even an exchange of surreptitious smiles
Will entail great risk. And say you will have noticed.

That being so, your fork will clatter to the plate. We'll be
Scrutinized, my co-smiler and I, and we'll be asked, What?

Except it won't be a question, really, because you'll know.
You'll know I wrote something, and you'll throw

Down your napkin and leave, and I might never see you again, though
Odds are I'll have found you at home hours later (I know better

Than to give chase just after ticking you off, contrary to the
Helpful *exempla* from heterosexual romances), and I'll try

To explain. I might even take the unprecedented step
Of showing you this poem, directing your swollen eyes

To stanzas twelve through fourteen, in which I declare my love
Of eating together in no uncertain terms (I hope you will have

Liked the part about the cereal bowl, which has a certain
Humble veracity), and we'll patch it up, slowly, as

We always have. If I knew what's good for me (if!),
I'd stop writing this poem now. Better still, I'd erase it

Altogether and occlude its awkward future. Clearly, that hasn't
Happened (either my knowing what's good for me or my making

Erasures, except of infelicitous formulations), because you have a little
More to read ("You" not necessarily being my wife, though if

You are she, it means I've had to show you this
After the Incident, for which I apologize again); and I,

From where I sit, a little more to write. I'm a fast eater, born of
Fast-eating people. Which is not to say we made

No conversation or had no pleasure as we inhaled
What was laid before us. But it is to say that mealtimes in our working-

Class household were functional affairs, that function being: to eat,
No, to finish eating in a timely fashion and to move on

To whatever activity came next, such as tetherball. (Never mind
When we had company and languished at table over half

An hour! Such are the exceptions that prove the rule.) In
My eulogy for you, dearest, even as I will have

Tarred you with the slow eater's brush, I will have to
Confess myself a fast eater, having sat all too often

Empty-plated and dazed, waiting for you to reach the halfway point
Of your meal. I'll recount my anxiety at watching your fork

Meander (tra-la!) in meadows of salad only to emerge (oh, hell!)
Bare-tined. Or seeing it, having hit its mark, rise to your

Lips, only to be lowered still laden with greens. How next
Time I'd hunker down and take excruciatingly tiny bites, each morsel

Savored, its texture relished—which engendered even slower
Eating from you. Nothing for it but to clutch my barleywine

And maximize our gastropub residency. Maybe I'll augment
My eulogy with a hymn to the barleywine (as the grieving do):

Barleywine! Hoppy and heady, barleywine! Meady and
Murky, barleywine! Served in a snifter, barleywine!, *ad nauseam,*

Until a friend will have approached the lectern, cupped the microphone,
And cradled me, whispering: Dude, this is no good,

It lacks veracity... So here's something of truth, how brisk
Your own luncheon will be without you to linger over

The lousy sandwiches. Let's go out tonight, however long
Or late. Then, when I'm brimming with barleywine

                                        (barleywine),

Put me to bed.

TURNING POINT

My wife has a fantasy dog,
Chocolate lab, part husky,
Vivid like the fantasy role-

Playing campaigns of my
Awkward youth or rosters
Of fantasy football. How vivid,

I learned while clearing out
Some junk before the guy
Came to fix the plumbing:

Among pots and birdhouses,
A water dish and chewy toys.
Keep Coco's things, she called,

As if (A) Coco would miss them
And (B) he'd been here all along.
I imagined him panting,

Lapping the water, warming
Our bed. I hope someday
I'll meet this majestic beast

In the flesh, but the timing's
Never right—not like raising
Children, where rules are made

As you go. There's no reason
Not to hope, but who knows?
Forgive me this morbid tack

And going through my papers
Don't hold this up and say:
Here was the turning point.

II

TRANSITORY

To be in the Roman airport is not to be
In Rome. This rule applies to all airports,
At all times, with the exception of

Vegas: Having flown through McCarran,
You've as good as been to the Strip.
There're big salads at Fiumicino Airport,

Pizza and coffee and gelato and
The Japanese, all essential ingredients
Of Rome, but the ratio is wrong,

And not even stunning backlit photos
Of the Forum or the Colosseum
Can put it right. When the day comes

That you take the commuter train
To the Roman airport, they spare you
The big sights. How miserable

To coast past St. Peter's or the Pantheon
Or even Mussolini's Typewriter
As you leave for good! I stood up

When we passed the Porta Maggiore
And the Baker's Tomb, grey marble
Clashing with deep copper bricks,

Forever partners in a squalid quarter.
I remembered everything it took to get
The students there, a forced march

Along the Via Giovanni Giolitti,
Not a gelato in sight, and little else but
Railroad tracks, cables, and traffic

Grazing narrow ribbons of sidewalk—
All of this to visit a hole in the wall
And discuss how good infrastructure

Is silent until it suddenly fails to work,
The way a body is healthy until it isn't
Anymore. I kissed my family goodbye

At Fiumicino, watching them go through
The checkpoint, waving in an obvious way,
So the security officers would understand

I wasn't waving at them. There're columns
Here at the airport, but they're ironic,
Made of welded steel. There're tiles

On the floor, but they're only vinyl.

ZANZARA

The mosquitoes of Rome find me
Delicious, as I find Roman cuisine.
I woke and saw the Big Dipper

On my forehead and cheeks, handle
Bent and a hole in the kettle.
I tossed my room hunting that

Mammone, bloated and punch drunk
On authentic American blood:
No trace but the grim constel-

Lation spanning my face. I told
A student I'd been brawling in
Bukowski's Bar. He didn't believe me

Even after I socked him on the arm.

LA PIETÀ

The virtue of the number 280 bus
Is its reach, cutting the Roman center
In two, north to south. Yet its virtue is
Its vice, because it stops everywhere
For everybody—democracy on wheels,

But a lumbering, lurching congress.
These are days so baroque
It hurts to think, much less walk.
Yesterday I lowered my gaze from the city
And put my forehead

On a pane of moving trees
And riverbanks. I opened my eyes
At Piazza Cavour and turned around
In time to see a man of sixty
Helping his mother, wrapped in a

Nonna sweater, her legs ending in
Nonna stockings and shoes, step down
Through the open doors and
Onto the pavement. They might have
Danced that way once, a slow waltz

At a wedding or a christening, when he
Was a child. His smile never faltered
As he lowered her into his arms
And made her to stand with dignity,
The pair of them a city

Unto themselves, looming
In the wake of the number 280 bus.

MY ELEVATOR, MYSELF

Caro Signor Ascensore,
Thank you for raising me up
To four, where I belong. You
Lack air conditioning and are
A sauna in the early afternoon,

But you exist; more than this,
You function. There are exactly
One hundred and three steps
In this palazzo, which I employ
Religiously, especially when

Jaunting down to one for the
First cappuccino of the day. But
Sometimes I need a *tiramisù*,
And here our priorities are mis-
Aligned. We're never on the same

Level, and when you arrive
You're packed with *ragazze*
Dressed to murder the Roman
Night. What crimes did you
Convey, such that they had to

Fit you with a camera?
Your walls display helpful
Warnings about ebola, and heaven
Forfend I hang a wet towel
On your railings and pay the

Penalty! You must resent our
American numbering. When I press
Four, do you mutter *Tre*
Under your breath? I'll cherish
Above all those early

Morning hours, when I slip
From my room in pajamas and
Sandals and take you down
As far down as one can take you,
To the courtyard and the fountain.

The only sound the sound of water.
The nebulous, brilliant sky.

RUINATION

On the regional from Salerno to Paestum,
After missing our bus and
Cramming our poor selves in,
Locals embarrassed and apologetic for the baggage
Littering the aisles and all the open rancor
(It's the weekend, the weekend!),

Two gypsies appeared and began
To strum and sing a melody
Aching and true,
Their voices a balm on the rash afternoon.

Thus Orpheus broke the great sinners of Hades.
Vultures lifted beaks from Tityus' entrails.
Ixion's wheel wound down.
Danaids dropped empty pitchers.
Tantalus was satisfied.
One might've deemed them all

Happy in that moment, listening,
A sliver of solace from eternal
Drudgery
            —but one would've deemed wrong,
For as great as their relief was, greater
Was their resentment of its passing,
The old tortures resuming. Better
To have heard nothing at all!

The car fell silent as the gypsies crooned,
Most of us fumbling for change.
I wanted to ask the song's name,
But they'd already moved on to the next carriage
And left me broken in half

The rest of the day. My wife said
We should've bought the special passes
So as not to have missed the bus
In the first place. I'm sorry, darling,
To have robbed you of an extra hour
With your temples. Hopefully

What you married will be ruin enough.

LETTERS TO *LA PORTINARI*

The church of Margherita dei Cerchi
Has baskets overflowing with epistles
To Beatrice. It might seem kind of jerky

To rummage through them as I did, but this'll
Make up for my transgression: I would rather
Be made to eat a *tiramisù* of thistles

Than violate the secrets of a lover.
I'd never touch a letter folded tightly,
But those I did were easy to discover,

Their pages introverted only slightly
Or not at all, the better for a nosy
Flaneur of middle age to treat them lightly.

Of these one seemed a boy's request (I suppose he
Was such, if not a hipster with an earring
Or else a laxbro waxing proud and prosy)

Committed to the paper after hearing
Of Dante's love for B., a reverie worth
Rehearsing for its honesty so searing:

Dear lady,
What's being dead like?
You're kind of famous
Now because of your ex-lover.
If I could have a
Happy and long life,
That would be cool.
(Signed) Mike.

O Beatrice, who gaze upon this crude earth,
Is he a genius or is he a wanker?
Would you in life have given him a wide berth

Or married him instead of daddy's banker?

ON THE JANICULUM

Monday evening, on our first bus ride,
I stole Alissa's camera. How could I not
When it begged to be plucked

From her pocket? Smile, I said
And snapped a few shots of her
Smiling before she got wise and began

To frown. On Wednesday the bus repaid me
By refusing to open its doors: Me and Alissa
Trapped inside, while outside the lucky

Refugees made sure to take our picture.
Jackie led after we crossed
The Tiber, while I hung back to herd

Stragglers: *Photographicus interruptus*!
Escaping Trastevere's maze, we ascended
Via Garibaldi, where we took our first

Long draughts from a Roman fountain.
You first! they cried, as though I meant
To poison them. The cool water soothed

My sore throat. On the Aventine, nine
Days later, the orange garden's fountain
Run dry, we stole refreshment

From shade and silence. Upward and past
The apocryphal square of Pietro,
Our goal: the Acqua Paola and its

Celebrated vista. Friday night, Sasha would visit
And grace us with her poems. She'd sing
The cemetery mornings and the sunset hour,

When the rooftops blaze like live coals. First
Monday was cloudy, but we were on fire
For the city below.

CARYATID NOIR

It's not easy being a fountain in a
City teeming with fountains. Take

This one in the Piazza dei Quiriti,
A square devoted (like all of Prati)
To the sons of Romulus. But the

Fountain here bespeaks the work
Of women. From a shallow pool

Surges an enormous mushroom
On a stem of acanthi, tips curled
Like O'Keefe petals, and ringed

With budding bowls to catch
The water from above. A naiad

Quartet adorns the cap, crouching
Back to back, nude but stern, their
Heads supporting a tortoise-shell

Basin that culminates in a pinecone.
Sleek limbs help to bear the burden,

Though sometimes an arm at rest
Clutches a divine ankle. In any other
City such a fountain would stop

Traffic. Here, engulfed by cypress
And umbrella pine, it escapes notice.

But the goddesses, who watch the
Crossroads, see everything. They've
Seen the republic's baby steps

And the years of lead. They saw me
Bumbling in search of coffee and

Batteries. They understood me
Before I got the idea, two weeks on,
To celebrate them in verse—as if

They needed celebrating anymore
Or even a kind word.

IN LUCCA

In Lucca everyone's name has two Cs
Like Puccini, who was born there and
Has his own gelato flavor, so you know
He's arrived. In Lucca everyone
Rides bicycles all the time, cars being

Banned from the city center. They litter
The sidewalks, the bikes, and no one
Ever chains them up: Who would steal
A bike in a town full of bikers?
Vittorio De Sica gets no traction here!

In Lucca you see the bikers coming
But you rarely hear them from behind,
Unless their riders mutter *permesso*
Or ring their bells, lucid dings or
Dull dacks if the chime is off-kilter.

Children of Lucca learn to pedal before
Learning to walk and have special seats
On their parents' bikes, where they read
Maps and shout directions, navigating
Themselves into productive adulthood.

The city of Lucca is surrounded by walls
Built for an invasion that never came.
(And by that token they did the job.)
Now they are public trails where all
Luccanesi spend their time in exercise

And Americans go to feel bad about
America. We rented bikes in Lucca and
Sailed around the ramparts like
The Sound of Music. My father-in-law
Broke into song, a kid again,

Riding his three-speed across town
To the dime store or the outskirts
Where the river meets the quarry.
The afternoon winds picked up,
But the rain held off—a stroke of

Good luck in Lucca.

CAFFÈ CORRETTO

Roman coffee is a tall tree
That keeps on climbing.
It doesn't need much, but

Sometimes they see fit
To correct it with liquor:
Sambuca, maybe, or grappa.

We savored our corrected
Coffees, understanding
They were the last pair

We'd take together. After
The shuttle took you
Away, I slowly gathered

My things, enough to earn
A trip to the corner bar.
The milk in my cappuccino

Was sweet, but the cup
Was all wrong.

MIXOLOGISMO

My boon companion exhaled

Seeing cocktails served at the wine bar.
He rejoiced finding in our bartender,
Davide, a tireless didact on the history
Of bitters.

       Just as Michelangelo
Created man and named him Davide,
So Davide mixed drinks heedless of name
From liquors of rhubarb and elder and
Davide-knows-what else, shaken until
Frothy as Tyrrhenian foam with
The might of Neptune himself.

               After these
Epic gestures, the humble pleasures of
Figs, cheese, and homemade bread.

We divine such things, but we rarely
Keep hold of them, ephemeral like the zest
Davide applied to our glasses, burnishing
Brim and stem:

         The scent of citrus ran
Riot at first then diminished, until only
The image of lemon, an after-fruit,

Ripens in groves of memory.

THE ART HISTORIAN'S REVENGE

I ought to become a talk-show host.
I think I'd be good. It took only five
Minutes for the art historian in the

Seat next to mine to spill her guts.
She said the last time she'd been
To the Vatican, her husband took

Her by the hand on a bench in the
Cortile della Pigna and proposed
Divorce—this after a day of her

Playing tour guide and leading him
From beautiful thing to beautiful
Thing, and finally to Beauty itself,

Only to exit the tacky gift shop
Of Truth. Soon she'd revenge herself
Twice over: on the papacy with a

Prestigious grant, and on her ex
With a fiancé, due to arrive three
Weeks from now. I took her card.

I had mine printed years ago, but
Forgot them as usual. I never expect
To meet anybody, I said.

MARE NOSTRUM

Summer came early to the shore
Today, a mosaic of bikinis and
Trunks and coolers and towels,

A vivid, tremulous museum
Of flesh—though my display
Was closed for renovation.

I walked shoeless through hot
Sand and stood on the ocean
Threshold, the waves soothing

My feet. My friend wanted
A chair and umbrella, so we
Moved one beach over,

No longer teachers, only
Tourists renting a piece of sea
And sky. He read his anthology,

I listened to music and dozed,
Both of us dazzled by luxury
And missing our women.

III

THE CONTINENTAL BREAKFAST

While she brushed her teeth, I said,
Look for an apple up to your standards.
If they have such an apple
Please bring that apple to me.
If they have a breakfast sausage sandwich,
Bring me a breakfast sausage sandwich
And forgo the apple. If you should
Do this for me, I would call you Goody,
Which is short for Goodwife.
I proceeded to nuzzle her neck.
She closed her eyes as though asking,
How the hell did this happen?

BEING BACK

Being back is more than reversing
The steps taken when going away.
I couldn't be back unless I
Came back, just as I went away

In order to be away. Your constant
Notes from London—helpfully signed
"From London"—made us dream of your
Drowning in the Thames and the chance

To miss you properly. Informing us
Of your return spoils your being back,
Like *arancini* plucked from the oil
Too soon. Being back is more than

Vetting strange currency, which is done
After coming back. It's the shabby
Art of tumbling into my lover's bed
(Even if my lover is me) and waking to

Some old nuisance: whiskers at my
Temple, dust in my throat.

YES

My calendar says yesterday was
Our anniversary, not of getting
Married but of getting together,
Twenty-eight years to the day

You answered my ironic, seductive
Letter (reading which would nowadays
Pitch me from a bridge) with a
Note of yours that said, in essence,

Yes. We neither of us knew then
What this would entail, how just one
Yes leads to others and becomes
Habitual, which habit ought to be

Broken with a judiciously placed
No, that the next yes mean more than
Go ahead. I've been puzzling over
What separates one epinician poet

From another, how each might design
An anniversary card. Bacchylides
Would show a swarthy Syracusan
Driving a four-horse chariot to victory

On the outside, HAPPY ANNIVERSARY
CRAZY KIDS! on the inside. Pindar
Would also say HAPPY ANNIVERSARY,
But show Prometheus bound, the eagle

Gorging on what's left of his liver.

THE LOVES OF BARBER

He asked me did I know Madeleine.

I said: She was a lover of mine, but I was
Mistaken.

He said as of age forty-seven he'd had
But one lover, one point five if you counted
The one who left before they could,
You know.

I said: Best to round down. Besides,
You've been married a long time,
So what do you expect, anyway?
You ought to listen to Barber, a lover
Of women, a man of not inconsiderable
Prowess (told me so himself).

He said: Barber's full of it. If he's such a
Stud, how come he's always at home
Making tea and biscotti and shit?

I said: When I was seventeen it was
Nineteen eighty-four. The seventies
Were half a decade back down the road,
But it felt like hundreds of miles.
They were behind a wall. Woodstock
Was only fifteen years gone, but
It was like another century.

He asked did I know what Barber says
About the seventies.

I didn't.

They were the best time to lose it.

I said: Come on! Barber is, what, like
Three years older than us? What was he,
Thirteen? Who the hell loses it—

Depends,
He said. I knew a guy who lost it
At twelve on the golf course behind
His folks' house.

I said: Jesus Christ. I was twenty-one and
I thought the world was ending.

He said: Ah.
And he took a long drink of beer. Then:

I wonder if Barber means the seventies
Were more laid back.

Well, they were, I said, they were that.

THREE NOVELLAS

Story of a girl who doesn't realize her mother is really
Her older sister, and her little sister is her sister's daughter—
That is, her niece. Her older brother, meanwhile, is actually
Her father, but not the father of her older sister, whose
Mother, now deceased, conceived her by another man, also
Deceased but fabulously wealthy and famously married. He
Promised his mistress lifelong security in return for secrecy,
With the results we see: mother–sister, brother–father,
Sister–niece all chasing the money while conspiring to give
The girl a life without exploitation or gossip.
They've become deft at dodging her awkward questions
And learned to restrict her reading: no detective
Novels, no Orwell, and nothing by that prophet Sophocles.

Story of an old woman
Beset with dementia
Convinced she's a time-
Traveler. Sees in her
Reflection herself at
Sixteen wearing her
Mother's earrings to the
Spring dance. Excited
For the future, vows to
Leap forward and see
The promise of tomorrow
Not knowing she already
Has. Disappears one
Morning, a tremulous
Note beside her arm-
Chair: See you in time.

Story of a man too clever by half
Obsessed with the question of why
If fire is a metaphor of desire
It shouldn't work in reverse.
Crusades to invert the referential
Polarity. Remakes his hearth as his
Heart. Petitions school boards
To hold passion drills. Asks the cook
At the cookout to love his meat
Well done. Loses job calling in
Sick with burning desires of a hundred

And three. Amatory fervor repels
Family and friends. Too poor
To heat the house, dies of cold,
That is, the lack of love.

THE LOW THEORY

It was the big lecture, to which all the theorists came.
She (he) talked about the low theory and we
Authenticated from the back row, nodding at
Poly Styrene and the ending of *Fantastic Mr. Fox.*
We felt low as low theorists do and went out,
Got independently drunk because we weren't
Invited to the reception, no problem because
The booze was better from where we sat,
On low stools, dreaming of shows we wished
We'd been high enough to see: Elvis spinning
His wheel (a pure gimmick) or the genesis of
Billy Bragg's big ideas. Do you know the video
Where Kirsty MacColl puts an arm around him
While mouthing "sexuality"? It's not lowdown low,
But it's still the greatest thing and remained so
Even when round three stole our reason, not our hearts.
Never hearts. This is what it means being punk
Past forty: Store your ragged past in the garage,
Pay the mortgage, or stupid rent, but bitch loud
Until the check clears.

NOMENCLATURE

My gallery-haunting friends
Like to ask who's on the wall or installed
In the alcove, heads bowed low
To the placard:

               It's Teresita Fernández (e.g.),
Though in that instant Teresita herself
Will be in Brooklyn, gathering greens
At market or making galaxies
Of thimbles.

Such familiarity would've
Tickled a mimetician like Aristotle,
But the modern dropping of names
Is overwhelming. Watch me
Nod sagaciously, a finger
Grazing pursed lips:

               Ah, yes,
Franz Ackermann, of course he is!

All of this said, I'll never
Pass up the chance to
Trample the corpus
Of that minimal-
Ist bastard,

Carl An-
Dre
.

MATINEE

It was amazing, it beggared belief
When you reached for my pocket
And pulled out a dove, snapped its
Neck, lit it on fire so that it became
A vase of daffodils tended by bees,
Setaceous bodies shimmering with dew,
Which you set upon the audience for the
Sting. Screams gave way to laughter
As the swarm transformed into the
Mormon Tabernacle Choir at the
Hallelujah Chorus climax. They spun
On the spot like dervishes, robes flaring,
Became umbrellas, for which we
Tussled when you brought down
The rain, the droplets changing to
Feathers and coating our soaking skin.
Your white-gloved hands swept us
Into a basket, your voice cooing softly:
Thank you, thank you, my doves.

BLINDSIDED

I'm sorry, former student,
For saying I was pleased
To meet you, for not

Remembering you as I
Should. In my defense,
You missed a lot of class

(I checked my ledger)
And you were quiet,
Not to mention my nominal

Aphasia or that the time
I was your professor
Was a time I'd like to

Forget—nothing to do
With you, I should add.
But the plain truth is

You were sitting next to
My child, who long ago
Reft me of peripheral

Vision and left me a
Heliomaniac,
Eyes only for the sun.

BIRTHDAY ADVICE TO MYSELF

Drill holes after cutting the tenons, not beforehand,
If want the holes to align. Befriend as many artists
As you see fit, but never drink with more than two
At a time. All cats are feral, but not all cats are
Feral cats. All bats abhor injustice, but not all bats are
Batman. Telephones are almost certainly killing you.
Fight fire with poetry, save water for California.
Fight California with New York, and fight New York
With Brooklyn. When visiting the city, never look
Upward and gape and point: You'll block
The sidewalk and upset the natives. Rather, fashion
Your face into a mask of indifference, if not disdain—
For tourists, for New York no longer the glorious
Whore when you and yours were coming up
In the 70s—and keep walking past Katz's Deli.
Make friends with death, though not to the point
Where you have a key to her apartment and let
Yourself in to feed the fish; more like a Facebook
Friendship, with vital updates and chances to like
Celebrity passings. Punctuation is dying period:
Be arrested for someone else's cause, and be seen
Being arrested to help get the word out. Post bail
In pennies to show your contempt for The Man.
Cook your best dishes without recipes, so you'll be
Missed when you're gone. I tried to make his
Eggplant, someone will say, but it just wasn't
The same; or: I pine for his cauliflower tagine.
Realize your index finger will never be whole;
Write poems about the accident ten years on. Gasp
At how the smartest people do the dumbest things,
Then lick your wounds. Resist the impulse to compose
Didactic epics on the herding of goats; not that
You're not a goatherd (you're not), but the very topic
Is bottomless. Take every opportunity to touch
Your wife, for one day either she or you will be
Intangible. There's no weakness in apologies. Deploy
Them like knives against those who never say sorry
For anything: You'll disarm them believing they've
Got the best of you. Take them for everything.
Women are sacred, not to be asked if they have
The rag on, nor to be assumed to have the rag on
When they demolish your way of thinking. Be

Gracious: It's not as though the world turns well
Under the watch of white men. Avoid public displays
Of satire, which covers its tracks and is easily taken
For bad wiring. Write inoffensive tripe and put
The masses the fuck to sleep. Insert the f-word
To see if anyone's paying attention. The longer the poem,
The fewer the readers, the lesser the brou-ha-ha,
The smaller the poet. It's all about diminishing returns.
Contemplate Ann-Margret's iconography—That face!
That voice! Those legs!—inject her fabulousness
Into your everyday routine. Brush teeth
With jazz hands. Teach in profile. Undulate. Wear
No pants. Form a band and become rock stars. Buy
Dime-store wigs and shades and open for yourselves as
The Preteens with a sweet, all boy-band repertory.
Savor the earnestness of irony, how it becomes an end
Unto itself when practiced assiduously. If you cough
In someone's face, ask: Isn't it bubonic? When you
Turn up stupid, shrug and ask: Isn't it moronic?
If having a lazy Sunday, roll over and whisper:
Isn't it laconic? This is why you have no friends
Or you have too many (artists not included). No matter
How wisely you mentor, how many letters you write,
You might not get invited to the wedding. And just
As well, because no one wants to hear you sing
"Voodoo Woman" during "Bohemian Rhapsody." Don't
Microwave in plastic, if you can help it. Don't help
Anyone out of a microwave: Odds are they deserve
To be in there. Beware their desperate pleadings and
Get-rich-quick blandishments. Wear lederhosen at least
Once in your high-strung life. Yodel in the stairwells,
Those vast, reverberating stairwells (stairwells). Go
Alpine while you have the legs. Jump the last ship
Off this sickening glorious beautiful cancerous rock.
Your forties have become the long corridor between
The youthful self, whom you still expect to locate
In the mirror, and the elder self you've kept
At arm's length. You're at the other end now.
It gives onto a room with comfortable furniture
And a full bar. Why not have a look around?

A WINTER'S FALL

O Winter, how mild you are this year!
My song as I tramped the light snowpack,
The lunar halo waning westward
At dawn, headed out back to check
The propane tanks. So much for romance!
Hard snow became ice underfoot and
My legs took leave of the ground. Supine,
I took inventory of myself (a list growing
Larger each year) and decided the pain of
A bruised hip was preferable to dying.
It would've killed my father, such a fall,
As would've the torment of being betrayed,
From which I've only begun to recover,
Spending the year fat and less sober
Than I wanted, but less drunk than needed,
A state of mind Father would've fathomed,
A state of body, too, at times in his life
Though not now, I'm told, with his precarious
Thinness. It's my extra padding spared
Me broken bones and imposed crystalline
Clarity on a winter's fall. Did Father's
Mishaps prompt a philosopher's turn?
Almost certainly, else he would never
Have been my father.

IRISH WAKE

We pallbearers eyed the coffin,
Estimating its weight versus the
Distance to the hearse. Jeffrey,

Suicidal but still with us, said
What we were all thinking as,
Arms aching, we lumbered

Down the stairs of St. Kate's:
Jesus, Grandma! Everyone had
An eye out for Dennis, who'd

Gone underground a decade before
But, staying gone, ruined our fine
Rebukes. I don't remember whiskey

At the house, but it couldn't have
Failed to be invited. Meanwhile
In the back bedroom, we played

Grandpa's siren as if besieged,
Its strains shattering our collective
Childhood. Mrs. O'Donaghue sang

The praises of passing in one's
Sleep: Holy Mary, that's the best
Way to go! It was the last time

We were all together, and nobody,
Nobody had a camera.

FOR PIERRE MACKAY

in memoriam

This, Pierre, was not what I wanted: pithy,
Elegiac sentiment, clipped and mannered.
You're too big for that. You were always too big,
   Bursting with data,

Like the office that barely held your projects,
Which I helped you clear. In a nondescript box
Was the world's first Arabic font on punch cards,
   Tossed in the trash bag

With a shrug: Oh, well. When we made papyrus
And arrayed the strips perpendicularly,
We concealed them under the heavy plaster
   Venus de Milo,

Inattentive to the Seattle climate
And the reek. They say you went gently, eyes closed
Over Sunday's crossword, without so much as
   Dropping your pencil.

DAVID,

The last time I saw you
Was between books in the library
Stacks. You didn't notice me
As you sloughed off to Latin
Or to meet Herb
At commons, where you and he
Insisted on eating during lunch rush,
Arms folded, a pair of ninnies
Waiting for a table, scowling at
The Sixties and the death of faculty
Privilege. I should have cleared
My throat or headed you off
But we'd only just talked
The year before.
My story of metamorphosis
Hadn't changed a whit,
And you looked so tired,
Still in your fifties but seventy-eight
In alcoholic's years. I took in
Your tobacco aroma,
Mingled with dust and pulp
From the volumes all around,
And loved you enough to let you pass.

UNCOVERING HOWARD

It seems to me now that Howard
Nemerov was pulling the strings
All along. He used to bait me
In graduate school, sneaking around and
Putting poems in my line of sight,
Like the time he took "To a Scholar
In the Stacks" and stuck it up
On a shelf-end at the University City
Library, knowing the classical
References would hook me,
First try. I saw him there often,
A jean-jacketed hobo who'd
Nod and smile at me in passing,
Waiting for me to catch on.
Meanwhile, there was that retro-
Spective of his time as P. Laureate,
Which showcased some of his
Original manuscripts, typed up
On butcher's paper, memoirs of
Commentary he was obliged
To provide on, say, "Casey at the Bat";
A resilient bit of doggerel,
I think he called it. I finally put face
To name at my commencement,
Where he was an honored guest
And read a poem. He winked at me
As I crossed the stage—no,
He handed me the diploma,
Clapping me on the back with
Those hoary Russian mitts. Howard
Never died that year, as was reported.
Rather, he followed me from
City to city. He cut our baby's
Umbilical cord, and later settled
An insurance claim in our favor
After the accident outside the house.
I know he folds my undershirts
And leafs through my chapbooks
When I'm not around. He clears
The cache on my browser, and I'd
Find him in the attic with a cup
Of coffee right now if I bothered

To throw open the door, but why ruin
A good thing? Destroy
The reputation of being dead he's
Worked so hard for? A quarter
Century's a long time to be away,
But formalism's a bitch like that,
Then as now.

MANORIST MODERN

On the airplane I kept the shutter half-
Closed, the half-sun illuminating

The dust rising from my shirt and me
Holding my breath. Later I blew on the

Cobweb, caught in spotlights like an
Escaped felon, dangling from the art

Collector's ceiling. He was possessed of
So much he needed notes to keep it

Straight, and even then the artists got
Heaped into a pile of bisexual guys,

Really nice folk. It was his wife's
Passion (he said) made their house a

Gallery over time, now (he didn't say)
A shrine to her eclecticism. I supposed

The oxygen tank had belonged to her,
Too, the object nearest his bed. Mean-

While the web danced in the unsettled
Air. I was drinking, but so were we all.

ELEGY #56

Of the things we still do together in bed
I don't sing. Let the muse close her legs

And recall for me the songs we sang
As newlyweds long ago—"Breaking Up

Is Hard . . ." (kamma kamma) and "When Will I
Be Loved?"—working together side by side

Fumbling our way between unison and
Harmony, the end of solos and the start of

Sweet polyphony. There's no sharp line
Dividing when we used to sing in bed and

When we stopped, no *terminus post quem*
Like 9/11 and waking up next day

To a changed world. I think it took years.
The singing grew ever sparser until it

Was a thing living only in past tenses.
Perhaps it's time to revisit the past,

A matter of lying down, caressing her
Shoulder, softly, bravely striking up

An old tune in the hope of reclaiming
The urgent, innocent why of it all.

TOWARD A GRAMMAR OF DEATH

A. Noun phrases
Death usually subject:
   Death is inevitable.
   Death comes to us all.
Some make death an object.
See also:
       Jesus, celebrity.
As indirect object, infrequent:
   Following the cotillion,
   Marie consigned François to death.
Death as possessive:
   The hand of death,
   At death's door.
Possession of death, obsolete.

B. Verbs
To die in any tense is plausible.
The future is preferable:
   I will die,
   You will die...
   They will die.
Modals often negatived:
   I can't let you die!
   I won't!
To die is active.
The passive is judged to be dead.
The subjunctive might be dead.
The gerund is dying.

C. Syntax
Death as abstraction;
In usage, unambiguous.
Prone to vocatives, irrational imperatives:
   O Death, pass over me!
   Cried the plummeting aviator.
Fluency is not competency.
Isolating structures, complex sentences.
Should death be subordinated,
The condition is temporary.
See also:
       alchemy, Eurydice.

Dan Curley grew up loving Greek mythology, which became a gateway drug to
Latin, which turned him into a serial classicist. Curley is an associate professor
in the Classics Department at Skidmore College. His teaching and research
interests include ancient tragedy, Latin poetry, and the classical world on film.
He is the author of *Tragedy in Ovid: Theater, Metatheater, and the Transformation of
a Genre* (Cambridge University Press, 2013) and a forthcoming textbook on
classical myth in cinema. His interest in poetry has been lifelong. For years
he taught and wrote about other people's poetry, but never gave much thought
to writing any himself, his days as a garage-rocker notwithstanding. Things
change, and somewhere along the line, like Juvenal, he got tired of being just
a listener. This is his first book of poems.

The cover was designed by S.L. Johnson.
Book title is set in Archivo Black.
Author name and blurbs are set in Times New Roman.

The interior was designed by Sky Santiago.
Poem titles are set in Trump Medieval.
Body text is set in Marion.